FARM PUZZLES

HIGHLIGHTS PRESS

Honesdale, Pennsylvania

Welcome, Hidden Pictures® Puzzlers!

When you finish a puzzle, check it off √. Good luck, and happy puzzling!

Contents

Cover illustration by Mark Corcoran

On the Farm

hockey stick

pencil

carrot

nail

crescent moon

artist's brush

ring

sock

ice-cream bar

candle

spoon

mallet

coat hanger

banana

5

Illustrated by R. Michael Palan

Greener Grass

teacup

musical note

paper clip

ice-cream cone

heart

banana

mitten

toothbrush

saw

fish

mushroom

artist's brush

6

Hello, Horses

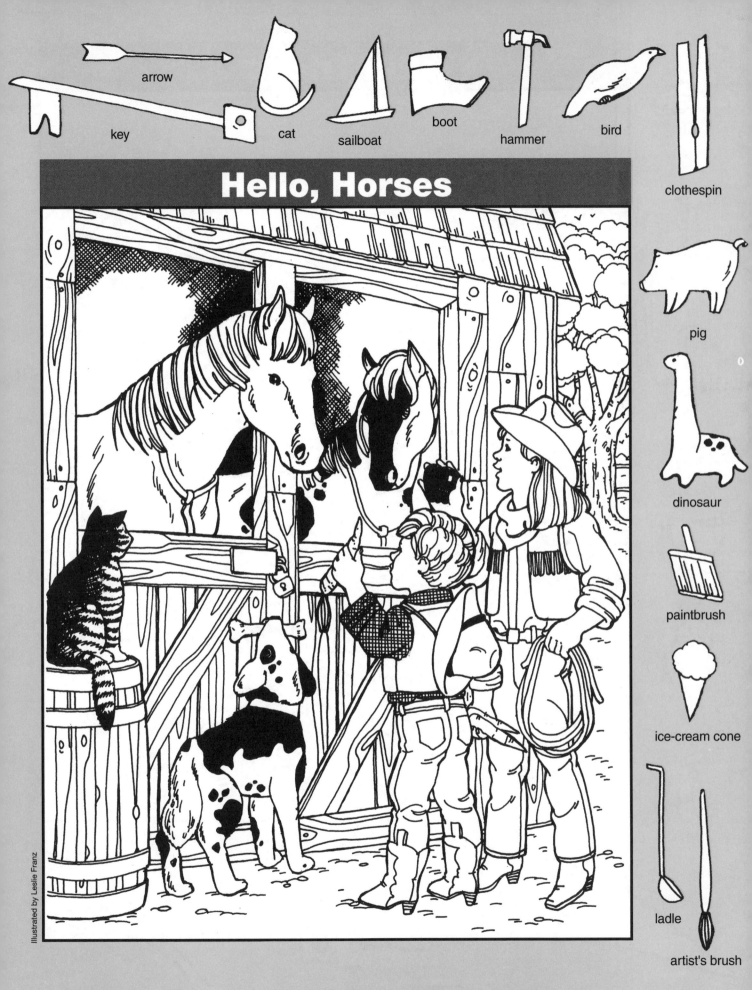

arrow

key

cat

sailboat

boot

hammer

bird

clothespin

pig

dinosaur

paintbrush

ice-cream cone

ladle

artist's brush

Illustrated by Leslie Franz

Pig Tricks

fish

hammer

nail

teacup

mitten

candle

pencil

heart

envelope

saw

ladle

2 buttons

Illustrated by Ron Lieser

8

sailboat

hat

telescope

fork

fish

ice skate

wedge of orange

bell

hoe

toothbrush

pencil

carrot

seal

spoon

candle

bow tie

slice of pie

firefighter's helmet

slice of pizza

cotton candy

screwdriver

screw

shovel

boot

Lots of Llamas

Illustrated by Linda Weller

9

bell

Fruits and Veggies

comb

pennant

chicken

brush

frog

book

heart

pencil

Illustrated by Ellen Appleby

ring

mitten

ruler

11

Do-Si-Do

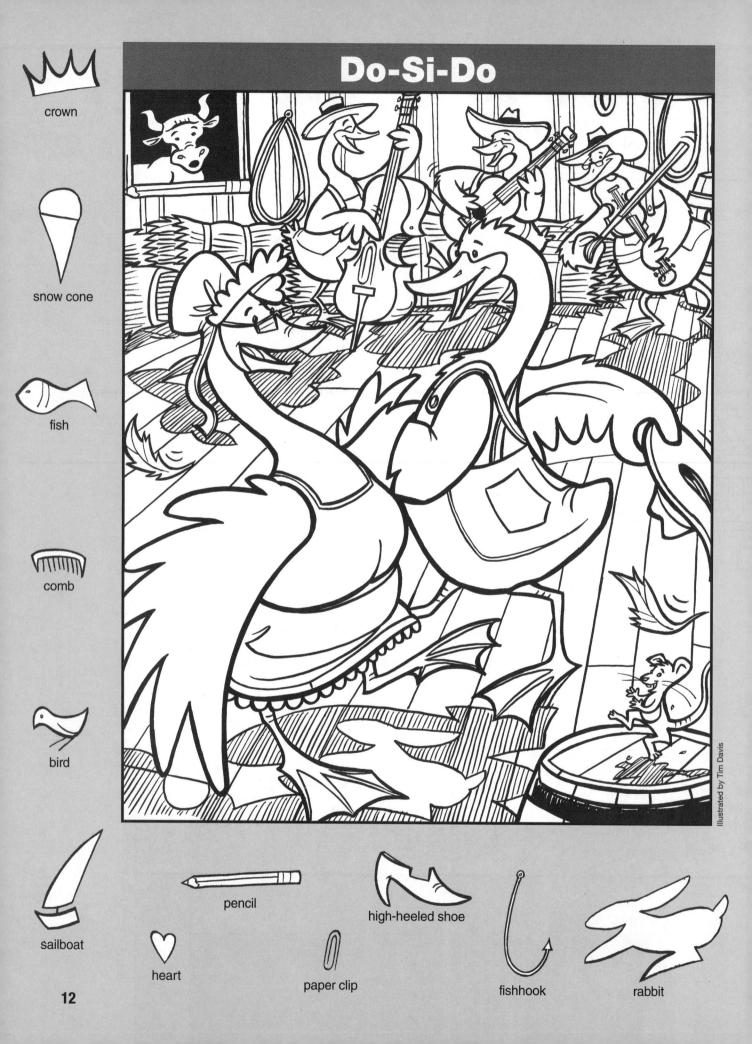

crown

snow cone

fish

comb

bird

sailboat

pencil

high-heeled shoe

heart

paper clip

fishhook

rabbit

12

Illustrated by Tim Davis

trowel

rabbit's head

tea bag

celery stalk

chicken

wedge of lemon

chicken drumstick

sock

building

spatula

carrot

open book

banana

sheep

sailboat

flag

What a View

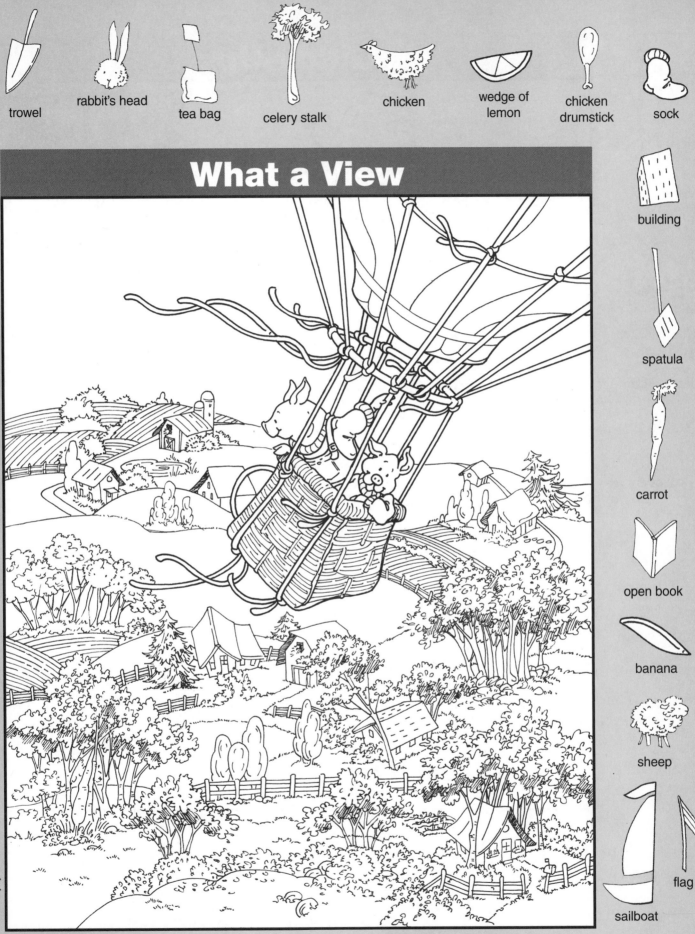

Illustrated by Lynn Adams

Giddy-Up

vase

spoon

paper airplane

cupcake

fish

jump rope

toothbrush

rabbit's head

hockey stick

pencil

necktie

cane

football

book

Illustrated by Patrick Coleman

14

hatchet

apple

two deer

fish

toothbrush

baseball

teacup

pail

bird

bell

bull's head

teapot

wooden shoe

bird's head

The Dog in the Manger

Illustrated by Jeri Simkus

15

Who Are You?

candle

eagle's head

broom

frog

screwdriver

porcupine

horse's head

hammer

pencil

butterfly

alligator

kangaroo

Illustrated by Kit Wray

16

The Scare-Rabbit

pig

butterfly

pail

boy's head

horseshoe

owl

2 birds

ax

hoe

dog's head

pencil

bottle

pitchfork

Illustrated by Mij Colson-Barnum

Swing Your Partner

banana

slice of pie

pen

light bulb

screwdriver

spatula

artist's brush

pencil

hoe

hammer

mitten

nail

golf club

paper clip

book

radish

bell

mallet

ladle

pushpin

slice of cake

needle

toothbrush

candle

Illustrated by Charles Jordan

19

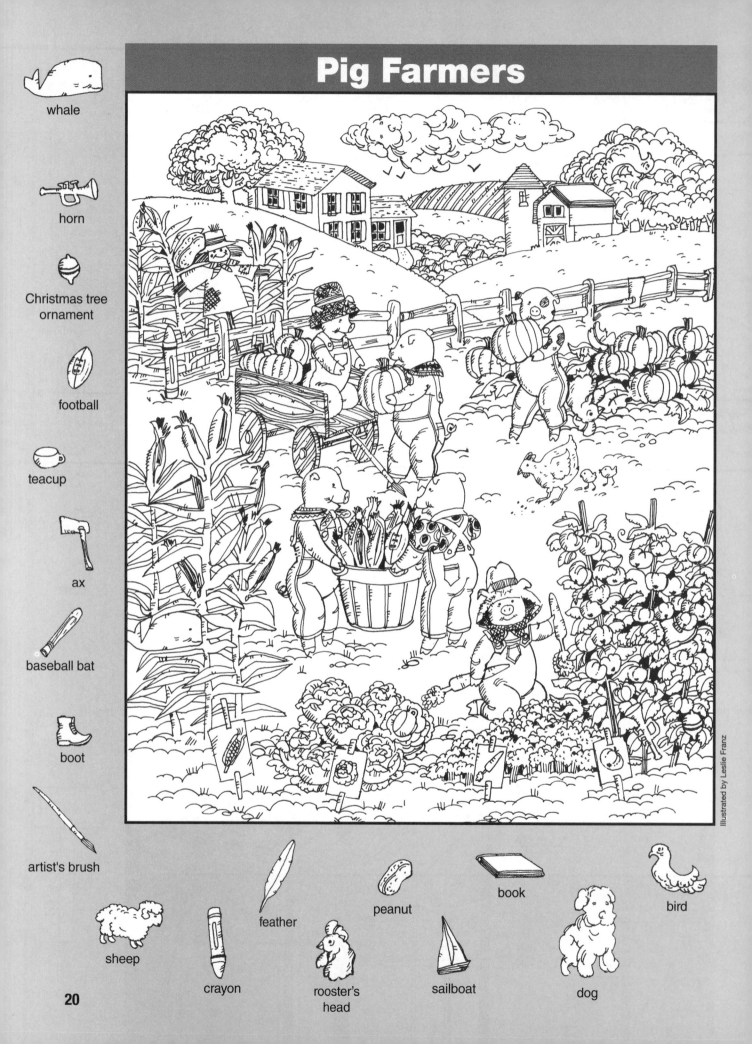

Pig Farmers

whale

horn

Christmas tree ornament

football

teacup

ax

baseball bat

boot

artist's brush

sheep

crayon

feather

rooster's head

peanut

sailboat

book

dog

bird

Illustrated by Leslie Franz

20

slice of cake

turtle

bird

teacup

carrot

camel

The Ugly Duckling

ice pop

chair

umbrella

buffalo

bear

Illustrated by Katharine Dodge

Time for Dinner

shuttlecock

octopus

bottle

pacifier

elf's head

doll

horse

bow tie

banana

boot

fish

Illustrated by Lucia Zacchi

22

wishbone

baton

fishhook

pair of pants

hammer

ice-cream cone

golf club

paintbrush

duck

pencil

open book

comb

pennant

fish

Country Hayride

Illustrated by R. Michael Palan

New Friends

candle

banana

hat

duck

open book

seal

mushroom

mallet

ladle

bird

boot

chick

shark

dog

24

Illustrated by Leslie Franz

open book

seal

teacup

pear

trowel

shoe

baseball cap

hammer

fishhook

sailboat

flag

needle

radish

ice-cream cone

paintbrush

spoon

Harvest Hoedown

2nd Annual Barnyard Jamboree

Illustrated by Holly Carryer

25

Flight School

pushpin

toothbrush

pencil

golf club

candle

teacup

slice of pie

open book

needle

dustpan

artist's brush

slice of cake

Illustrated by Charles Jordan

26

flag

pencil

needle

musical note

bell

mouse

boot

slice of pizza

snake

bowl

candle

top hat

apple

ladder

carrot

Milking Lesson

Illustrated by Janet Robertson

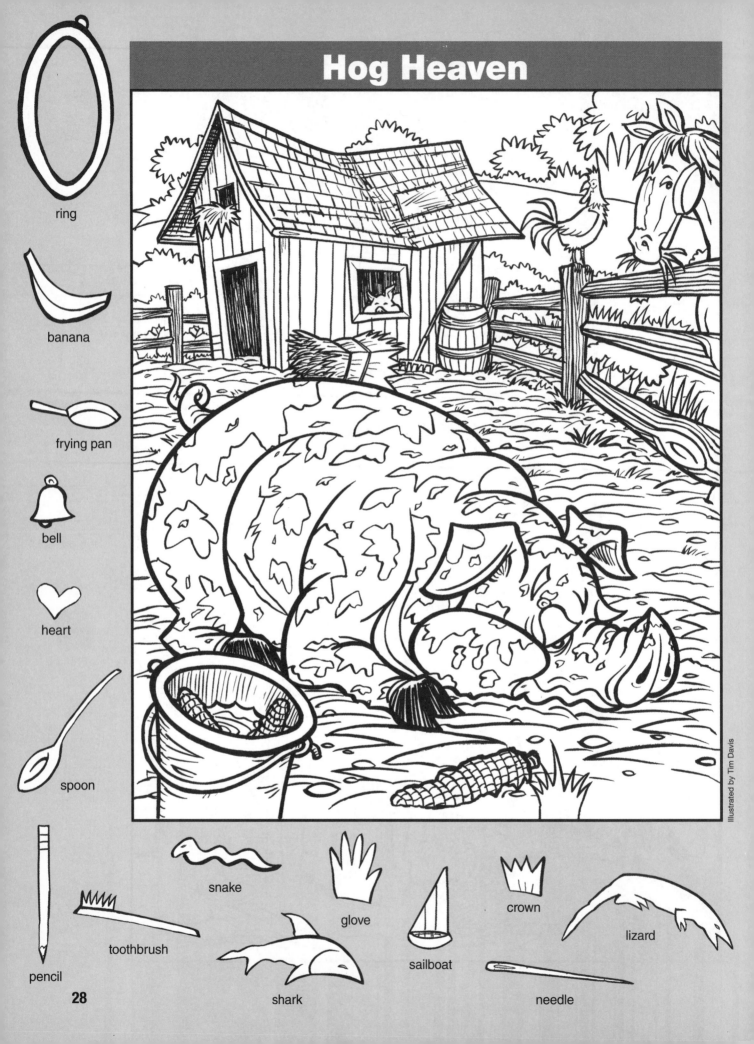

Hog Heaven

ring

banana

frying pan

bell

heart

spoon

pencil

toothbrush

snake

glove

shark

sailboat

crown

lizard

needle

Illustrated by Tim Davis

28

caterpillar

coffeepot

mitten

ruler

banana

screwdriver

shoe

Barn Dance

hatchet

kite

butter knife

funnel

crescent moon

Illustrated by Kit Wray

Bringing in the Cows

water pump

slice of pizza

carrot

coffeepot

screwdriver

owl

pitcher

chicken

cat

bird

chipmunk

seal

feather

light bulb

shoe

shark

30

seashell

mailbox

slice of bread

bell

fish

ice-cream cone

hammer

Illustrated by Linda Weller

candle

duck

rabbit

kangaroo

toothbrush

31

Slippery Shoats

gingerbread man

mushroom

key

shovel

party horn

eyeglasses

mouse

heart

toothbrush

high-heeled shoe

ring

dog

Illustrated by Tim Davis

32

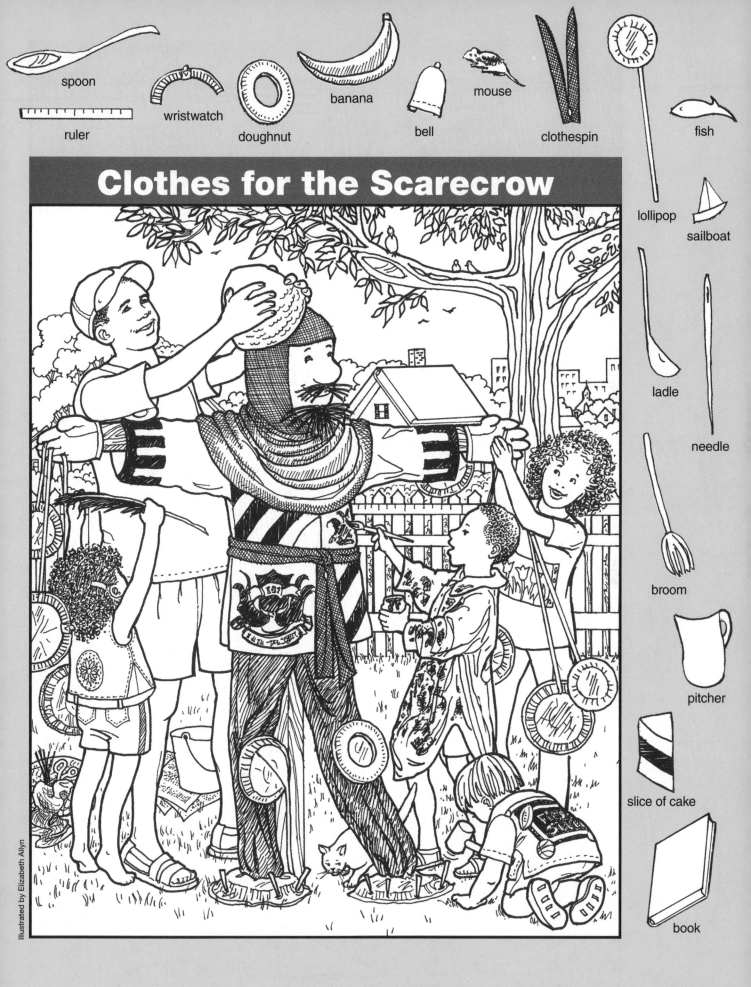

spoon

ruler

wristwatch

doughnut

banana

bell

mouse

clothespin

fish

lollipop

sailboat

ladle

needle

broom

pitcher

slice of cake

book

Clothes for the Scarecrow

Illustrated by Elizabeth Allyn

Rooster's Serenade

golf club

glove

heart

pencil

comb

paper clip

ice pop

rocket ship

artist's brush

banana

pine tree

nail

sailboat

megaphone

ice-cream cone

eyeglasses

dog

Illustrated by Tim Davis

34

Over the Fence

cat

paper clip

slice of pie

tweezers

sock

toothbrush

duck

heart

artist's brush

shovel

pencil

sailboat

bowling pin

Illustrated by Tim Davis

Piggy Pool

whale

screw

spool of thread

fishhook

pair of gloves

slice of pie

telescope

eyeglasses

rabbit

toothbrush

wishbone

screwdriver

mallet

flashlight

Illustrated by Cynthia Henstock

36

fishhook

candle

musical note

key

slice of bread

needle

snake

mushroom

shoe

crescent moon

toothbrush

nail

pencil

artist's brush

golf club

Garden Visitor

Illustrated by R. Michael Palan

Pumpkin Patch

crescent moon

sock

boomerang

banana

candle

butterfly

acorn

fishhook

toothbrush

teacup

screwdriver

needle

golf club

duck

38

ladle

ring

flower

fish

football

bell

pencil

spoon

hammer

snake

nail

rowboat

boot

Illustrated by R. Michael Palan

Farmer Mouse

pear

bird

candle

sock

crescent moon

boot

spoon

banana

artist's brush

turtle

tack

ice-cream cone

teacup

needle

caterpillar

Illustrated by Chuck Galey

40

pennant

musical note

trowel

slice of pizza

hammer

pen

hockey stick

winter hat

boot

teacup

crescent moon

ice-cream cone

key

Party Crashers

Illustrated by R. Michael Palan

Prize Pumpkin

milkshake

butter knife

pointy hat

needle

pencil

teacup

golf club

musical note

nail

toothbrush

spatula

crown

ring

slice of pie

Illustrated by R. Michael Palan

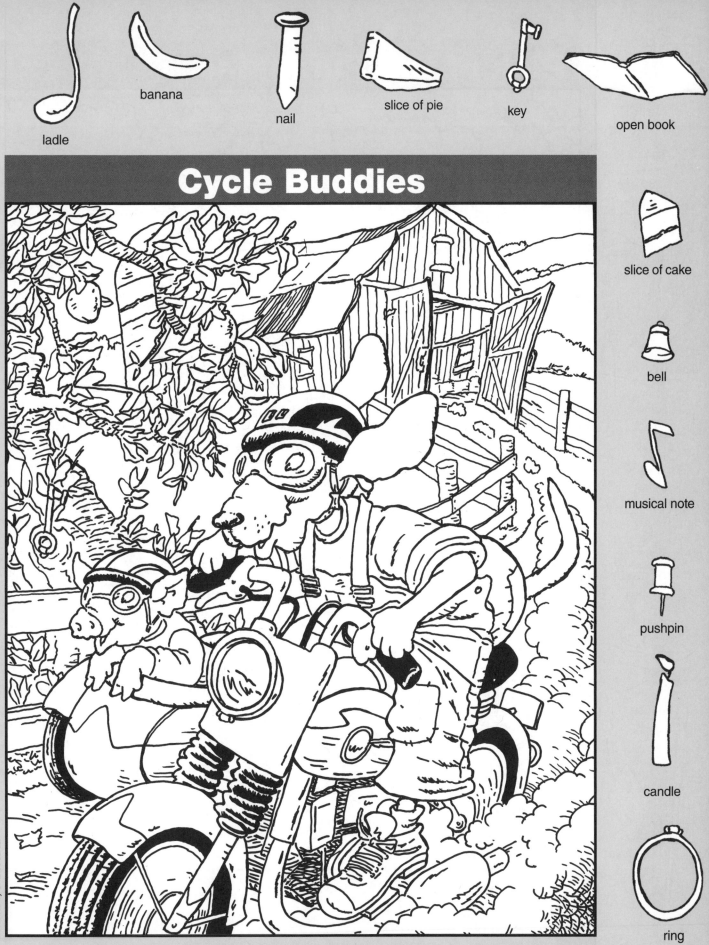

ladle

banana

nail

slice of pie

key

open book

Cycle Buddies

slice of cake

bell

musical note

pushpin

candle

ring

Illustrated by Charles Jordan

Pick of the Pumpkins

spoon

mitten

slice of cake

candle

mushroom

bell

shoe

croquet mallet

spatula

whistle

teacup

slice of pie

safety pin

pen

ring

broccoli

ice-cream cone

feather

tack

bike pump

carrot

hoe

toothbrush

pencil

Illustrated by Charles Jordan

45

Friendly Scarecrow

slice of cake

muffin

artist's brush

spoon

safety pin

golf club

slice of pie

slice of bread

ice-cream bar

candle

mushroom

shovel

Illustrated by Charles Jordan

dragonfly
eyeglasses
pennant
comb
fish
2 mice
duck
arrow
bird
turtle
sailboat
hammer
ice-cream cone

Billy Goat's Garden

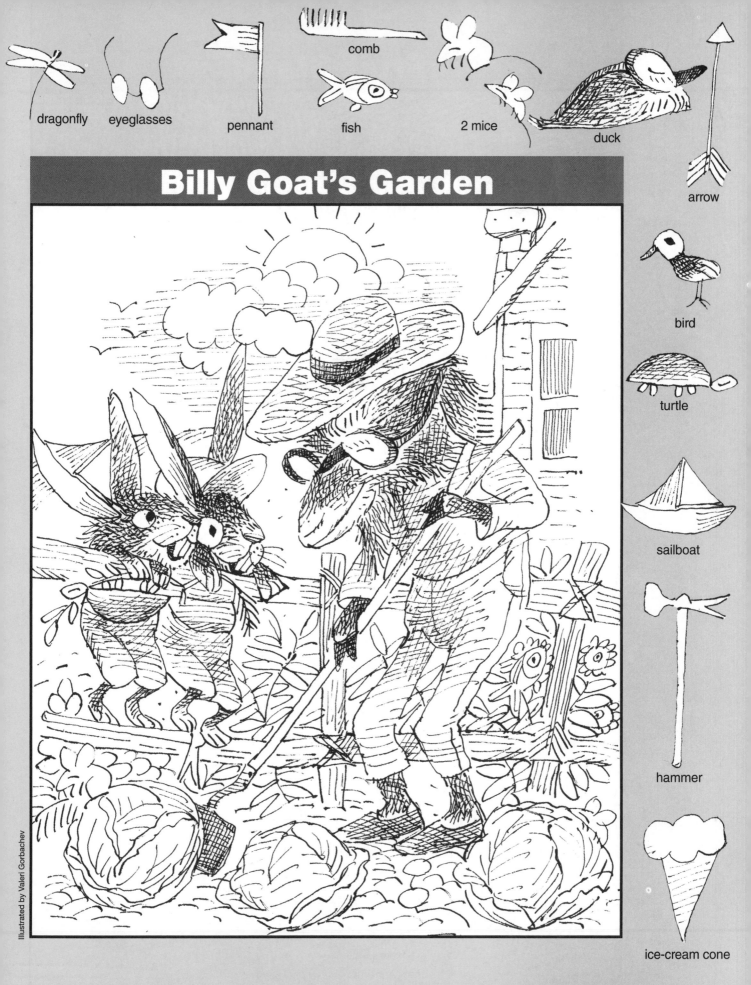

Illustrated by Valeri Gorbachev

Fruit Stand

heart

pencil

sailboat

crescent moon

hammer

pen

boot

bell

paper clip

candle

megaphone

carrot

eyeglasses

banana

comb

slice of pie

toothbrush

48

Illustrated by Tim Davis

chicken

bird

slice of pizza

bowling pin

pencil

elf's hat

mallet

crescent moon

briefcase

teacup

mushroom

feather

Wagon Serenade

Illustrated by Kit Wray

Nose to Nose

lizard

lantern

swan

juicer

star

tent

pie

toothbrush

bear

carrot

lamb

hat

cowbell

hammer

Illustrated by Mij Colson-Barnum

Unexpected Company

ice-cream bar

telescope

open book

lizard

candle

tweezers

carrot

pennant

mouse

funnel

two bells

teacup

Illustrated by George Wildman

Farmer Ants

teacup

lollipop

pencil

coat hanger

fishhook

spoon

toothbrush

needle

banana

nail

carrot

spatula

candle

UNCLE ANDY'S ANT FARM

Illustrated by R. Michael Palan

kite

bell

pushpin

cupcake

slice of pie

slice of cake

safety pin

golf club

magic wand

closed umbrella

candle

ice-cream cone

Summer Song

Illustrated by Charles Jordan

Fresh Picked

cane

magnet

crescent moon

cupcake

ruler

ring

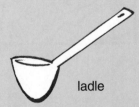

ladle

54

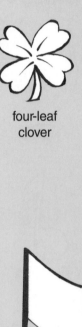

balloon

four-leaf
clover

flag

heart

funnel

bell

55

Illustrated by Rocky Fuller

Harvest Apples

mouse

candle

heart

banana

musical note

tack

toothbrush

crescent moon

mushroom

golf club

fishhook

crayon

teacup

flag

needle

nail

closed umbrella

snake

spoon

arrow

Illustrated by Sally Springer

56

ring

candle

ice-cream cone

key

comb

nail

tack

pencil

Down on the Farm

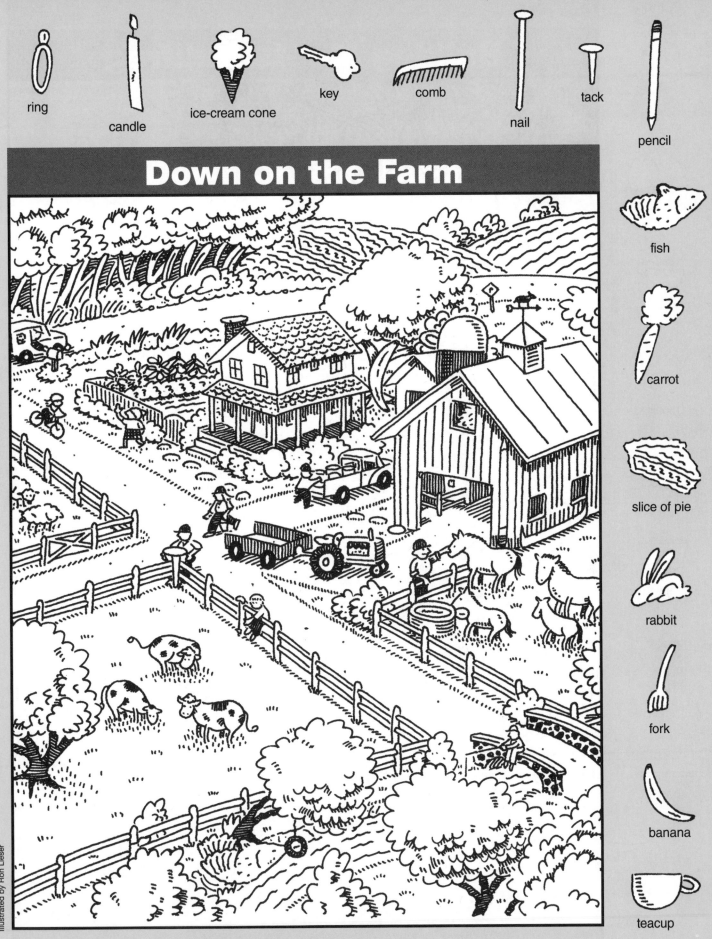

fish

carrot

slice of pie

rabbit

fork

banana

teacup

Illustrated by Ron Lieser

57

Bulldog Meets Bullfrog

bell

baseball cap

teacup

muffin

button

bowl

pennant

book

spoon

briefcase

needle

sock

carrot

spool of thread

pear

shuttlecock

wishbone

Illustrated by George Wildman

Garden Lunch

nail

banana

heart

fish

wishbone

ring

sailboat

musical note

pencil

cane

toothbrush

paintbrush

needle

slice of pizza

slice of bread

spoon

drinking straw

candle

LETTUCE

Illustrated by Sally Springer

59

Smiling Scarecrow

teddy bear

pennant

slice of pizza

teacup

golf club

two fish

sailboat

loaf of bread

toothbrush

shoe

saucepan

mushroom

bell

ice-cream cone

mitten

artist's brush

Illustrated by Maggie Swanson

Boxcar Racers

mallet

ring

slice of pie

safety pin

slice of cake

candle

mushroom

pushpin

spoon

golf club

magic wand

jump rope

Illustrated by Charles Jordan

Therapy Riding

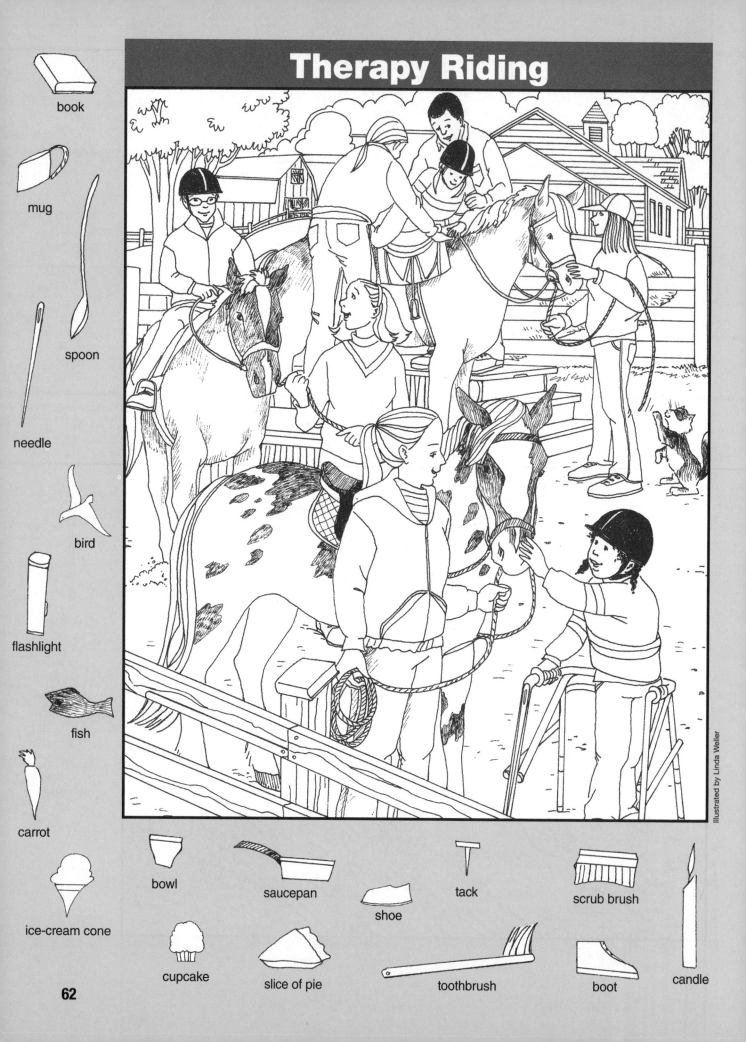

book

mug

spoon

needle

bird

flashlight

fish

carrot

ice-cream cone

bowl

saucepan

shoe

tack

scrub brush

cupcake

slice of pie

toothbrush

boot

candle

Illustrated by Linda Weller

62

Geography Lesson

clothespin

heart

spoon

artist's brush

sock

nail

duck

wrench

pear

comb

fish

seashell

pencil

teacup

glove

Illustrated by Ron Lieser

63

New Chick

toothbrush

funnel

glove

pencil

comb

arrow

horseshoe

key

eyeglasses

ice-cream cone

dog

flower

butterfly

disk

fish

64

Illustrated by Tim Davis

slice of cake

bicycle pump

saucepan

tack

book

ring

Flying Machine

pennant

ice-cream bar

candle

fishhook

carrot

pushpin

Illustrated by Charles Jordan

Square Dance

banana

pencil

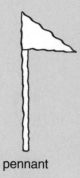
pennant

sock

book

ring

Illustrated by David Helton

kite

spatula

toothbrush

ruler

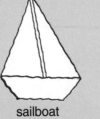

sailboat

button

Apple Picking

sailboat

mouse

mushroom

lollipop

crescent moon

wishbone

candle

swan

saucepan

teacup

toothbrush

bell

hammer

slice of pie

pitcher

fish

Illustrated by Linda Weller

scissors

mouse

slice of bread

hat

fish

heart

banana

shoe

candle

bowling pin

drinking glass

pine tree

The Little Red Hen

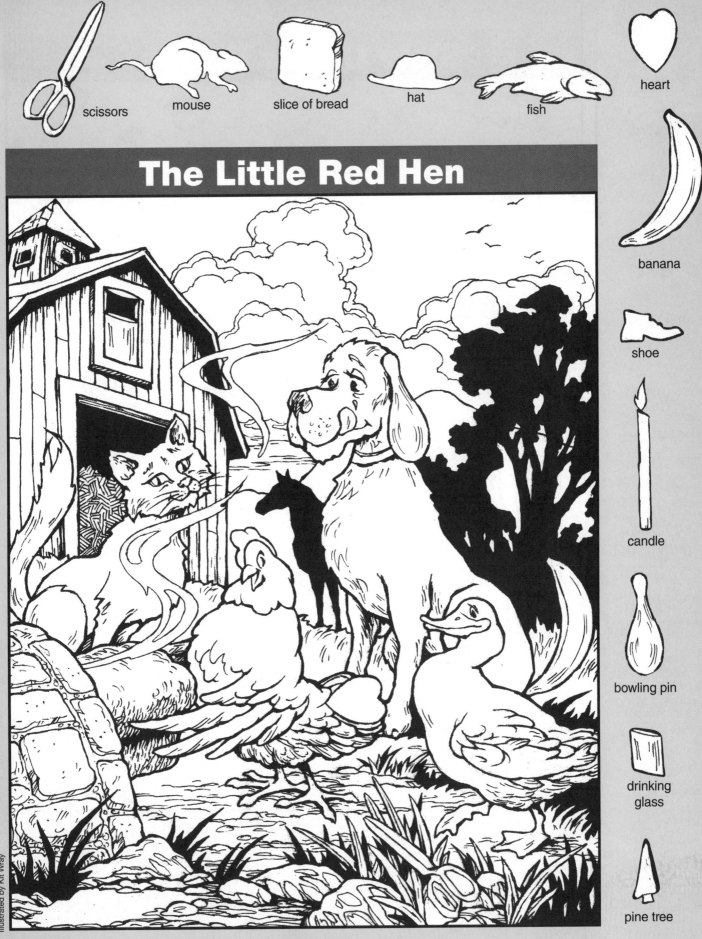

Illustrated by Kit Wray

Slow Up for Ducks

baseball cap

artist's brush

toothbrush

fork

ice-cream bar

carrot

candle

shoe

cupcake

cotton candy

crescent moon

pennant

Illustrated by George Wildman

apple core

toothbrush

spoon

slice of pizza

heart

baseball glove

open book

gingerbread man

teacup

banana

sock

fish

pencil

artist's brush

What's for Lunch?

Illustrated by Maggie Swanson

Hoedown

pencil

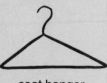

coat hanger

banana

glove

shoe

crown

72

needle

handbell

sailboat

toothbrush

ice-cream cone

carrot

73

Let's Play

bowl

artist's brush

teacup

candle

pear

pennant

book

ice-cream cone

umbrella

bow tie

needle

carrot

tack

Illustrated by George Wildman

fish

glove

bat

toothbrush

rat

heart

tweezers

hat

coat hanger

bell

sailboat

goose

Proud Parents

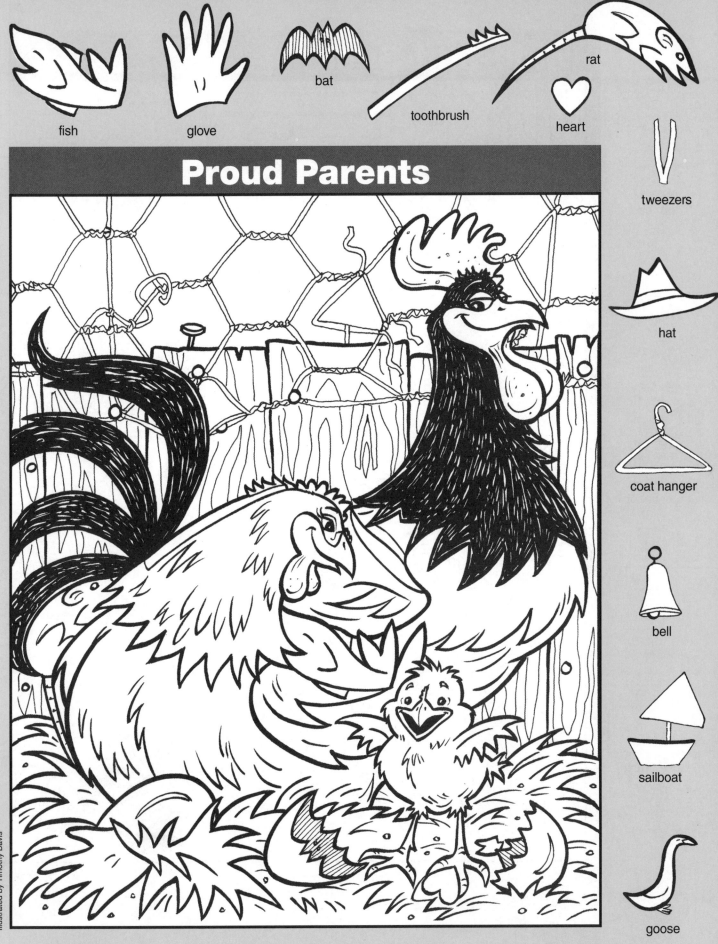

golf club

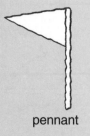

pennant

toothbrush

CD

ring

teacup

ruler

spatula

pencil

Illustrated by David Helton

slice of pie

book

envelope

A Drive in the Country

earmuffs

banana

toothbrush

teacup

ladle

pencil

penguin

mitten

sock

toy top

caterpillar

crutch

golf club

nail

pennant

needle

flag

Illustrated by Elizabeth Allyn Hendricks

78

mallet

carrot

artist's brush

toothbrush

ice-cream bar

bell

candle

pencil

nail

mushroom

ice-cream cone

bicycle pump

Heading Home

Illustrated by Charles Jordan

mushroom

crescent moon

sailboat

paper clip

mug

needle

slice of cake

apple

The Mule's Day Off

Illustrated by Rocky Fuller

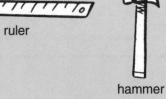

scissors

pennant

spoon

flashlight

ruler

hammer

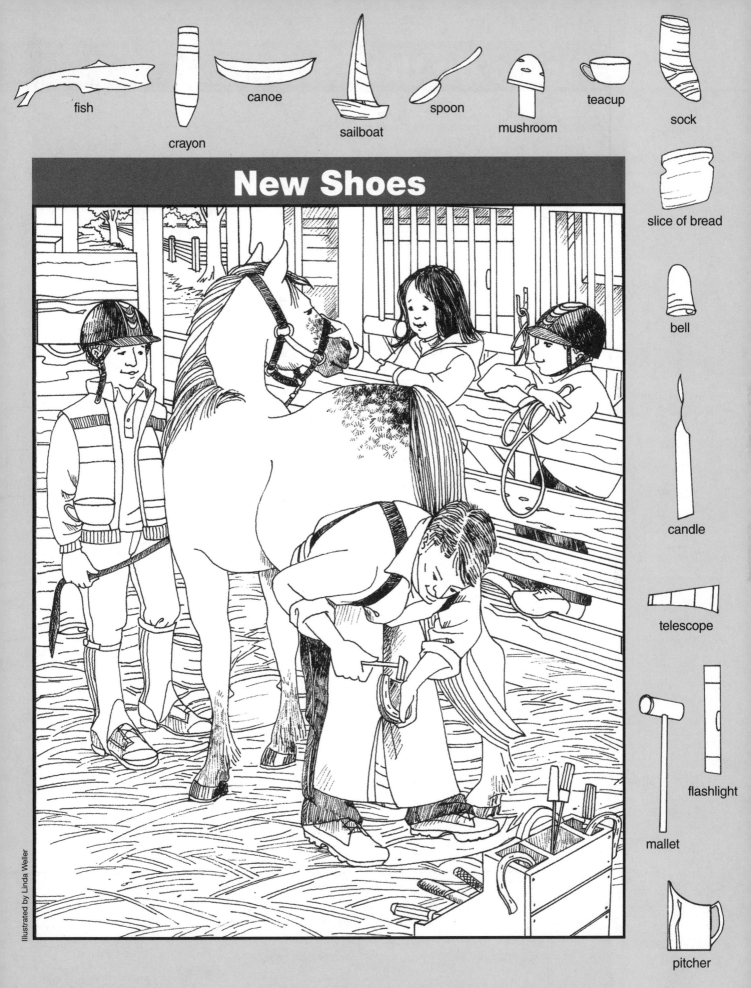

fish

crayon

canoe

sailboat

spoon

mushroom

teacup

sock

slice of bread

bell

candle

telescope

flashlight

mallet

pitcher

New Shoes

Illustrated by Linda Weller

Picnic on the Farm

heart

mallet

nail

feather

arrow

drinking straw

ice-cream cone

flag

bowl

crescent moon

pencil

banana

golf club

saw

mitten

mug

open book

shovel

toothbrush

spool

ice-cream bar

bell

canoe

Illustrated by Paul Richer

Life is Good

carrot

pear

toothbrush

hippopotamus

baseball cap

lollipop

needle

fish

bat

worm

snow cone

open book

slice of cake

Illustrated by Susan T. Hall

84

rabbit

open book

nail

bowling pin

toothbrush

seashell

fish

slice of pizza

cane

drinking glass

spoon

shoe

candle

light bulb

banana

pumpkin

carrot

Corn on the Cob

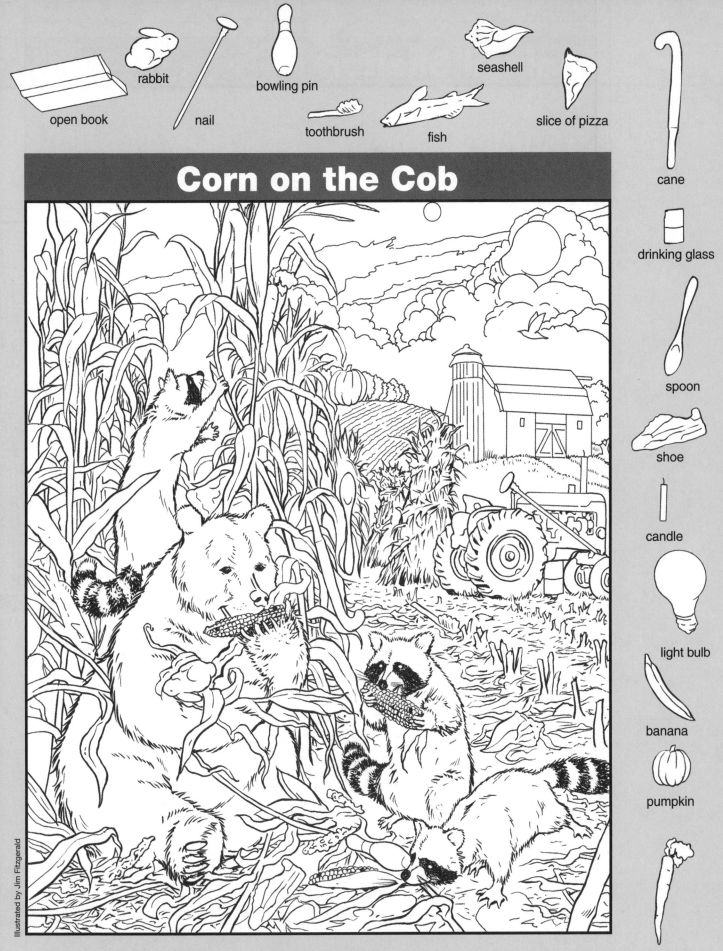

Illustrated by Jim Fitzgerald

Animal Shelter

pennant

domino

bow tie

doughnut

fried egg

chili pepper

sock

paper clip

belt buckle

kidney bean

adhesive
bandage

button

carrot

fishhook

mallet

ladle

safety pin

tack

candle

Buckets of Blueberries

feather

mitten

slice of cake

radish

shovel

Illustrated by Charles Jordan

88

candy corn

kite

pencil

book

fish

paintbrush

ring

flower

Band in the Barn

Illustrated by Susan Dahlman

sock

sea star

candle

spool of thread

slice of pizza

spoon

heart

CD

Time Out

open book

hamburger

drinking straw

banana

pencil

glove

nail

clothespin

carrot

mouse

candle

slice of pie

Illustrated by George Wildman

fish

flashlight

book

ice-cream bar

artist's brush

banana

tack

golf club

slice of cake

pushpin

mushroom

pen

acorn

celery

Stopping By

Illustrated by Charles Jordan

91

Fall Festival

pencil

open book

broom

ice-cream cone

drinking straw

spoon

ladder

glove

envelope

Illustrated by Ellen Appleby

sailboat

crescent moon

teacup

93

Hen Party

fish

ring

carrot

closed umbrella

fishhook

mop

horseshoe

butterfly

dragonfly

pen

pencil

glove

94

Illustrated by Chuck Galey

caterpillar

heart

envelope

bowl

ring

ladle

kite

fried egg

button

candle

dustpan

spatula

ruler

sailboat

Garden Goodies

Illustrated by David Helton

GATOR CABBAGES

seashell

open book

crescent moon

envelope

In the Pasture

handbell

spoon

heart

teacup

banana

light bulb

rabbit

key

flashlight

hammer

crown

baseball bat

Illustrated by Maggie Swanson

97

Fruity Fare

spoon

sunglasses

ladle

button

candle

bell

feather

sock

cupcake

golf club

spatula

ring

bracelet

envelope

ruler

Illustrated by David Helton

heart

crescent moon

ring

musical note

fish

screw

shovel

banana

drinking straw

light bulb

needle

doughnut

ice-cream cone

mug

crayon

October Bounty

Pumpkins and Apples for Sale

Illustrated by Jennifer Emery

Autumn Treats

banana

light bulb

mushroom

boot

crescent moon

envelope

sock

cupcake

pear

hat

horseshoe

mallet

seashell

airplane

ladle

glove

Illustrated by Arieh Zeldich

100

Stowaway Pilot

fish
slice of watermelon
broccoli
adhesive bandage
elephant
flag
pen
teacup
golf club
open book
crayon
needle

Illustrated by Susan T. Hall

Feeding Time

swan

candle

slice of pie

mug

golf club

handbell

sailboat

loaf of bread

spoon

hammer

horseshoe

pitcher

fish

shovel

Illustrated by Linda Weller

102

lollipop

fishhook

crown

mushroom

egg

slice of pizza

Down by the Stream

Illustrated by Maxim Mitrofanov

musical note

banana

heart

crayon

glove

artist's brush

Barnyard Dance

shovel

teacup

drinking glass

pear

tack

pumpkin

light bulb

envelope

pitcher

bell

crescent moon

boot

clamshell

hanger

cane

mirror

ring

key

banana

pineapple

ice-cream cone

hammer

boomerang

button

sailboat

comb

2 dominos

2 hearts

oar

Illustrated by Arieh Zeldich

Flying Squirrel

slice of pizza

balloon

open book

butter knife

jump rope

mitten

carrot

bell

snake

candle

ghost

wishbone

Illustrated by George Wildman

banana

carrot

pencil

pen

key

artist's brush

golf club

mallet

open book

tack

slice of pie

candle

Bringing in the Cows

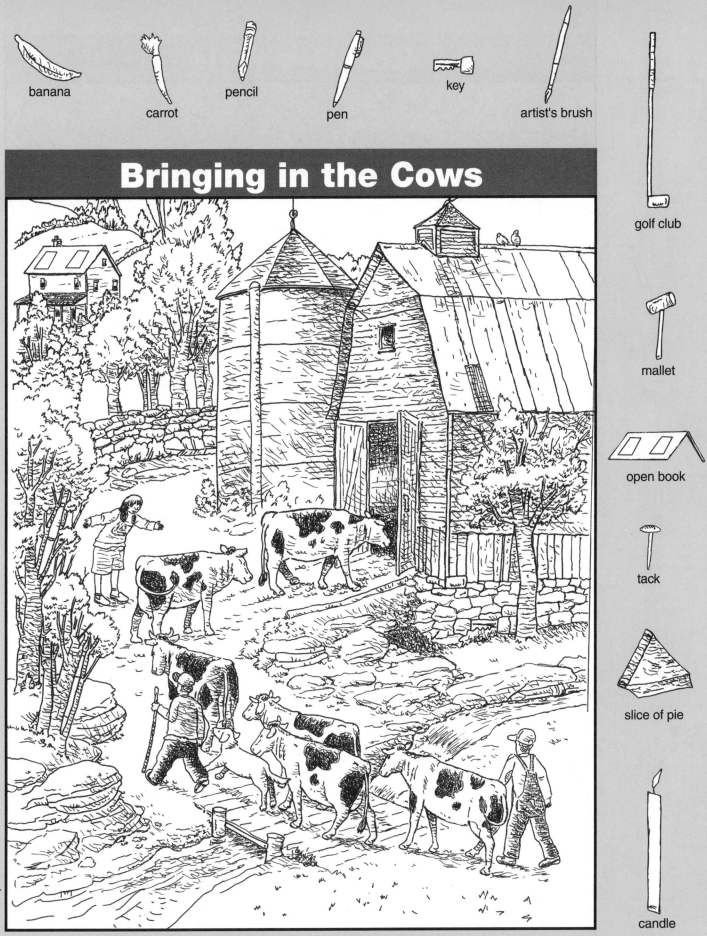

Illustrated by Charles Jordan

Country Ride

slice of pizza

spatula

needle

tack

nail

pencil

ladder

crown

ice-cream bar

book

mitten

comb

golf club

sock

Illustrated by R. Michael Palan

108

spool of thread

crown

acorn

ice-cream cone

party hat

envelope

fish

snail

mug

slice of pizza

canoe

pencil

teardrop

artist's brush

Farmers' Market

Illustrated by Gary Mohrman

carrot

slice of cake

bell

pushpin

candle

mushroom

needle

nail

slice of pie

spoon

wishbone

umbrella

Illustrated by Charles Jordan

110

butterfly

comb

ice-cream bar

scissors

wishbone

banana

mouse

Silly Not Scary

duck

carrot

glove

trowel

artist's brush

Illustrated by R. Micheal Palan

111

Horseless Carriage

baseball bat

fish

pencil

tweezers

shoelace

seashell

ring

open book

hat

pennant

mitten

slice of pizza

Illustrated by George Wildman

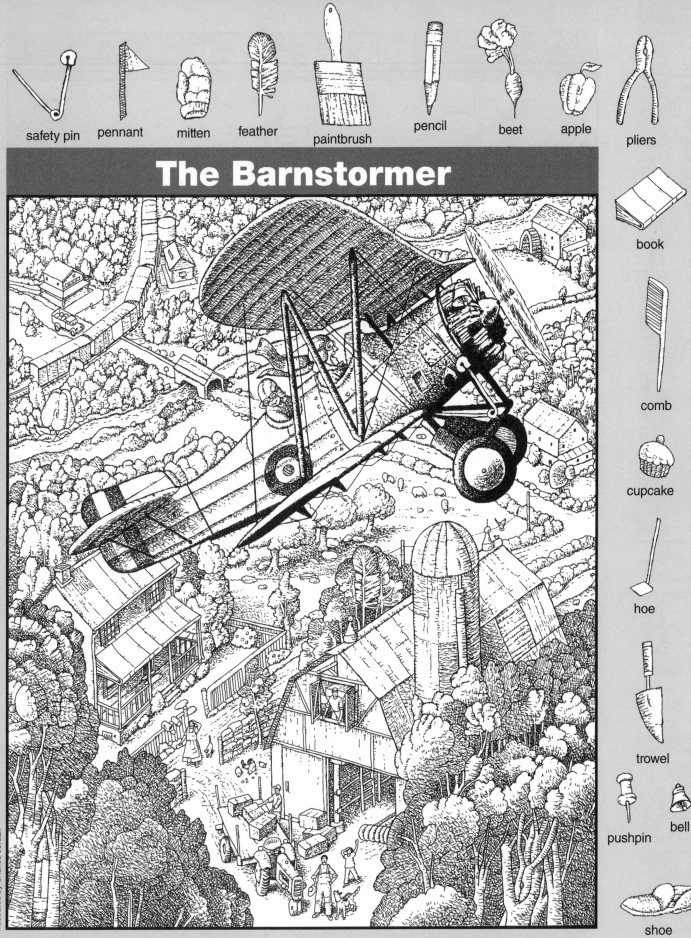

safety pin · pennant · mitten · feather · paintbrush · pencil · beet · apple · pliers · book · comb · cupcake · hoe · trowel · pushpin · bell · shoe

The Barnstormer

Illustrated by Charles Jordan

Pig on a Roll

heart

candle

mallet

ruler

key

ice-cream cone

banana

saw

wristwatch

glove

drinking straw

magnet

teacup

114

heart

saucepan

cane

doughnut

jump rope

slice of pie

Sudden Storm

party hat

flag

horseshoe

carrot

bird

open book

Illustrated by George Wildman

Rise and Shine

baseball bat

pennant

spatula

pencil

leaf

ruler

banana

envelope

fork

artist's brush

teacup

comb

116

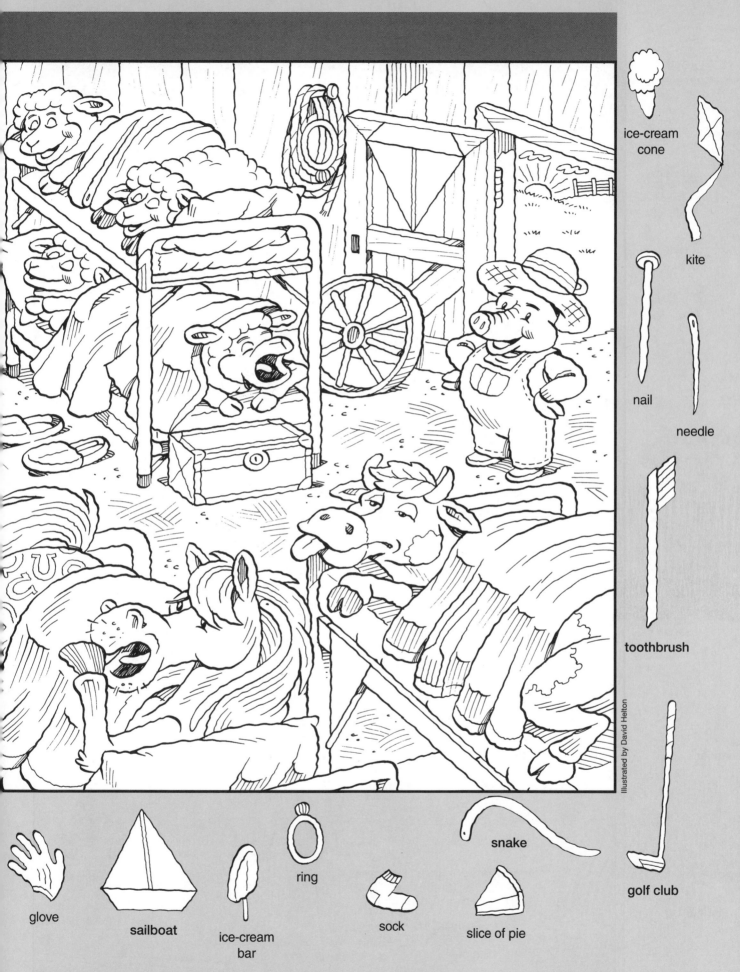

ice-cream cone

kite

nail

needle

toothbrush

golf club

glove

sailboat

ice-cream bar

ring

snake

sock

slice of pie

Illustrated by David Helton

117

Above It All

snake

hoe

golf club

kite

slice of pizza

stamp

ladder

ring

artist's brush

open book

boot

slice of pie

ice-cream cone

needle

flag

muffin pan

rake

Illustrated by Millard Hall

118

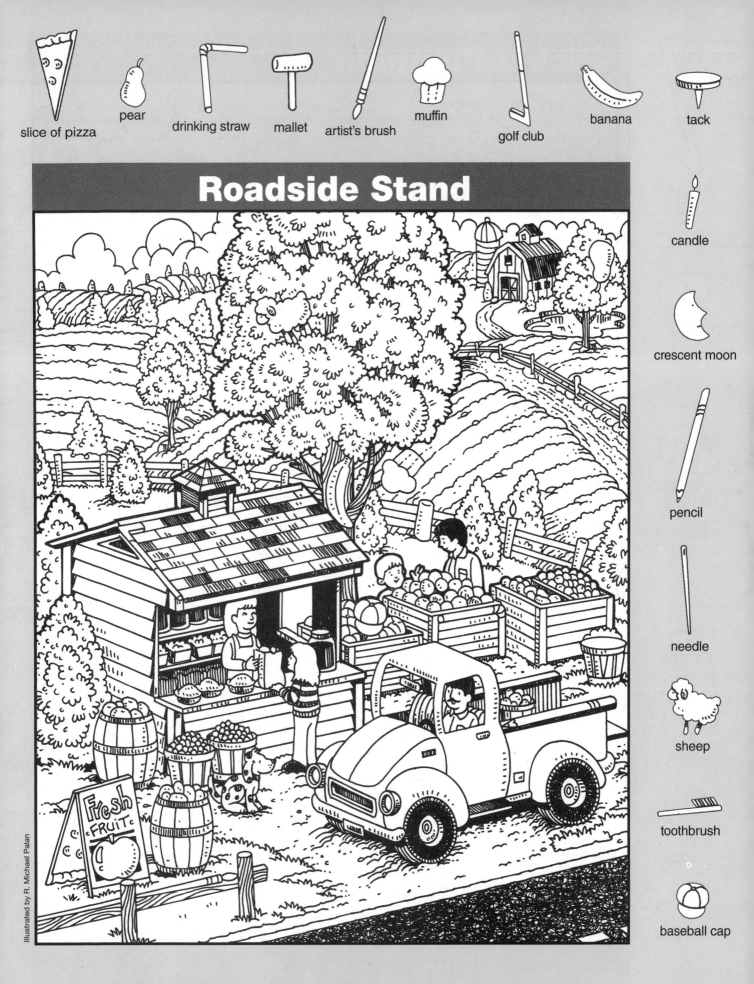

slice of pizza

pear

drinking straw

mallet

artist's brush

muffin

golf club

banana

tack

Roadside Stand

candle

crescent moon

pencil

needle

sheep

toothbrush

baseball cap

Illustrated by R. Michael Palan

Fresh FRUIT

119

Pick a Pumpkin

golf club

heart

ice-cream cone

stocking

boomerang

mushroom

crescent moon

orange

hammer

pennant

carrot

Illustrated by R. Michael Palan

bird

candle

crown

Farm Set

candle

coin

crescent moon

crown

ring

comb

key

drinking straw

caterpillar

slice of pizza

muffin

needle

thimble

clothespin

golf club

Illustrated by Ron Lieser

cinnamon bun
pencil
fish
pitcher
bell
pine tree
spoon
comb
artist's brush
baseball bat
vase
banana
heart
needle
feather

Apple Snacks

Patchwork of Farmland

domino

snowman

wedge of lemon

pencil

teacup

adhesive bandage

sock

crayon

ice-cream cone

fish

snake

ball of yarn

snow cone

party hat

slice of pizza

Illustrated by Susan T. Hall

tube of toothpaste

elf's hat

flag

caterpillar

tweezers

fishhook

ice-cream cone

heart

slice of pie

spatula

golf club

ring

feather

coin

key

toothbrush

seashell

button

Escape Goat

Illustrated by Ron Lieser

Bingo's Breakfast

magnet

pennant

clothespin

hammer

glove

comb

golf club

snake

pencil

piece of
candy

crescent
moon

candle

teacup

Illustrated by Ron Lieser

slice of pie

ring

saltshaker

bowl

sock

envelope

kite

banana

pencil

spoon

button

golf club

feather

flashlight

ruler

Sunflower Farm

Illustrated by David Helton

saw

seashell

clothespin

baseball bat

paintbrush

mitten

mug

shoe

envelope

Riding Stables

cherries

carrot

ring

spoon

pencil

canoe

light bulb

can

screwdriver

slice of pizza

open book

screw

artist's brush

ice-cream cone

rabbit

key

fork

crown

lemon

acorn

banana

candle

broccoli

heart

star

fish

Illustrated by Maggie Swanson

129

Answers

▼ Pages 4–5

▼ Page 6

▼ Page 7

▼ Page 8

▼ Page 9

▼ Pages 10–11

▼ Page 12

▼ Page 13

▼ Page 14

▼ Page 15

▼ Page 16

▼ Page 17

▼ Pages 18–19

▼ Page 20

Answers

▼Page 21

▼Page 22

▼Page 23

▼Page 24

▼Page 25

▼Page 26

▼Page 27

▼Page 28

▼Page 29

▼ Pages 30–31

▼ Page 32

▼ Page 33

▼ Page 34

▼ Page 35

▼ Page 36

▼ Page 37

Answers

▼Pages 38–39

▼Page 40

▼Page 41

▼Page 42

▼Page 43

▼Pages 44–45

▼Page 46

▼ Page 47

▼ Page 48

▼ Page 49

▼ Page 50

▼ Page 51

▼ Page 52

▼ Page 53

▼ Pages 54–55

Answers

▼Page 56

▼Page 57

▼Page 58

▼Page 59

▼Page 60

▼Page 61

▼Page 62

▼Page 63

▼Page 64

Answers

▼Page 65

▼Pages 66–67

▼Page 68

▼Page 69

▼Page 70

▼Page 71

▼Pages 72–73

Answers

▼Pages 74

▼Page 75

▼Pages 76–77

▼Page 78

▼Page 79

▼Page 80

▼Page 81

Answers

▼Pages 82–83

▼Page 84

▼Page 85

▼Pages 86–87

▼Page 88

▼Page 89

▼Page 90

Answers

▼Page 91

▼Pages 92–93

▼Page 94

▼Page 95

▼Pages 96–97

▼Page 98

▼Page 99

▼Page 100

▼Page 101

▼Page 102

▼Page 103

▼Pages 104–105

▼Page 106

Answers

▼Page 107

▼Page 108

▼Page 109

▼Page 110

▼Page 111

▼Page 112

▼Page 113

▼Page 114

▼Page 115

Answers

▼ Pages 116–117

▼ Page 118

▼ Page 119

▼ Pages 120–121

▼ Page 122

▼ Page 123

▼ Page 124

Answers

▼Page 125

▼Page 126

▼Page 127

▼Pages 128–129